I am a Great White Shark

Karen Durrie

www.av2books.com

AV² provides enriched content that supplements and complements this book. Weigl's AV² books strive to create inspired learning and engage young minds in a total learning experience.

Your AV² Media Enhanced books come alive with...

 **Audio** Listen to sections of the book read aloud.

 **Key Words** Study vocabulary, and complete a matching word activity.

 **Video** Watch informative video clips.

 **Quizzes** Test your knowledge.

 **Embedded Weblinks** Gain additional information for research.

 **Slide Show** View images and captions, and prepare a presentation.

 **Try This!** Complete activities and hands-on experiments.

Go to www.av2books.com, and enter this book's unique code.

BOOK CODE

D213883

AV² by Weigl brings you media enhanced books that support active learning.

... and much, much more!

Published by AV² by Weigl
350 5th Avenue, 59th Floor New York, NY 10118
Website: www.av2books.com   www.weigl.com

Copyright ©2013 AV² by Weigl
All rights reserved. No part of this publication may be reproduced, stored in a retrieval system, or transmitted in any form or by any means, electronic, mechanical, photocopying, recording, or otherwise, without the prior written permission of the publisher.

Library of Congress Cataloging-in-Publication Data

Durrie, Karen.
 I am a great white shark / Karen Durrie. -- 1st ed.
      p. cm. -- (I am)
 ISBN 978-1-61913-223-8 (hardcover : alk. paper) -- ISBN 978-1-61913-224-5 (pbk. : alk. paper)
 1. White shark--Juvenile literature. I. Title.
 QL638.95.L3D87 2013
 597.3'3--dc23
                                                            2011042348

Printed in the United States of America in North Mankato, Minnesota
1 2 3 4 5 6 7 8 9 0   16 15 14 13 12

012012
WEP060112

3 5944 00124 3532

Project Coordinator: Karen Durrie   Art Director: Terry Paulhus

Weigl acknowledges Getty Images as the primary image supplier for this title.

I am the biggest fish in the ocean that hunts its food.

I have skin that feels like sand paper.

I do not have any bones in my body.

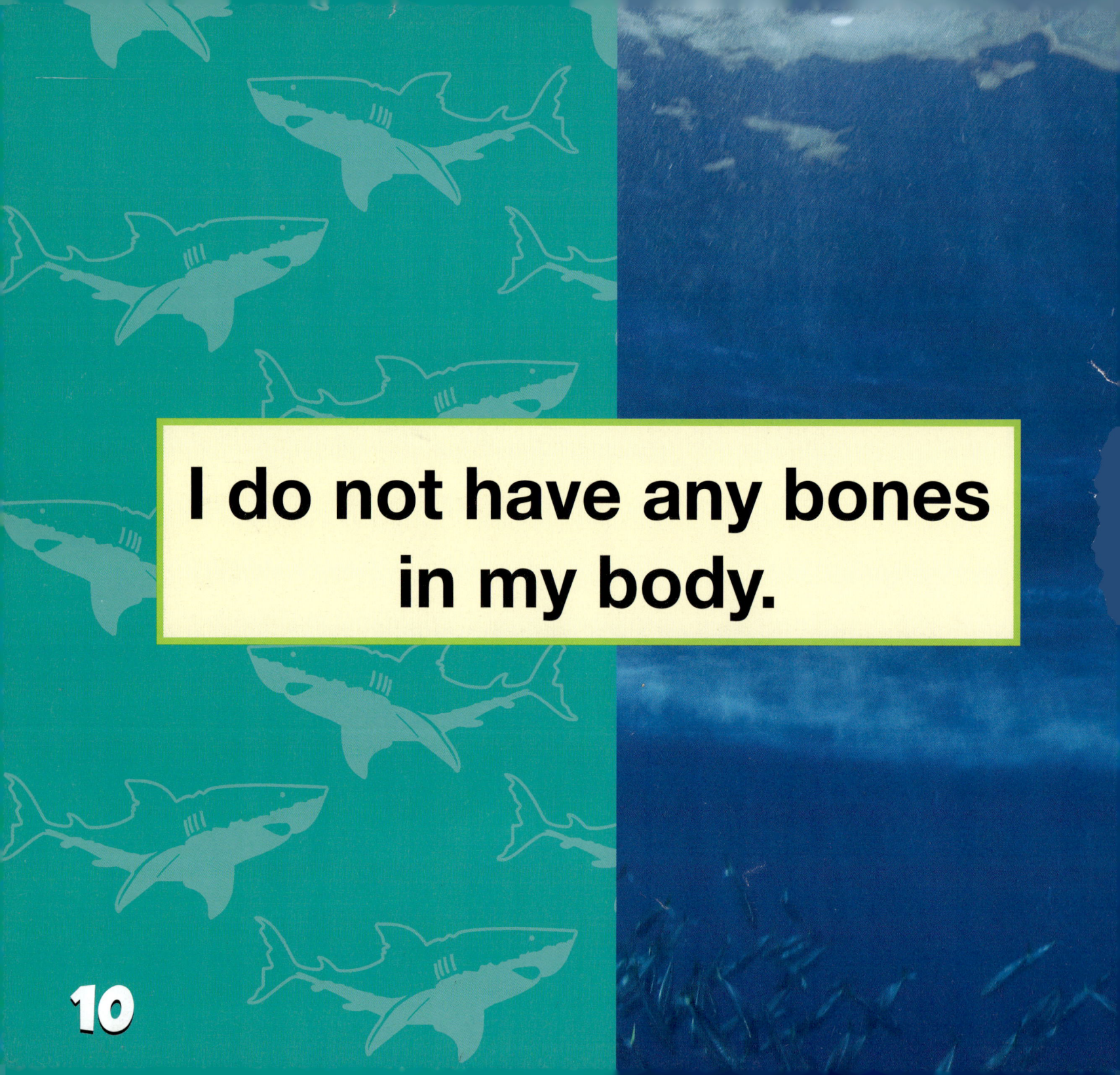

10

I can smell
one drop of blood
from three miles away.

I can swim when I am asleep.

15

I grow new teeth all my life.

I can find a heart beat from 9 feet away.

19

I have a big fin on my back.

I am a great white shark.

20

SHARK FACTS

These pages provide detailed information that expands on the interesting facts found in the book. They are intended to be used by adults as a learning support to help young readers round out their knowledge of each amazing animal featured in the I Am series.

Pages 4–5

I am a great white shark. Great white sharks live in coastal waters in oceans all over the world. When they are born, they are called pups. They swim away from their mother right away and look after themselves. Great white shark pups are about 5 feet (1.5 meters) long.

Pages 6–7

Great white sharks are the biggest fish in the ocean that hunt food. Great white sharks are the biggest predatory fish on Earth. They can reach more than 20 feet (6 m) long, and can grow to more than 5,000 pounds (2,268 kilograms). This is as heavy as a pickup truck.

Pages 8–9

Great white sharks have skin that feels like sand paper. The great white shark's skin is covered with a layer of tiny teeth called denticles. These denticles make the shark's skin feel rough, like sandpaper, in one direction, but if touched in the other direction, the skin feels smooth.

Pages 10–11

Great white sharks do not have any bones in their bodies. A shark's skeleton is made of cartilage. This is the same as the bendy material that makes up the flexible part of people's ears and noses. Cartilage helps sharks to turn quickly when they swim.

Pages 12–13

Great white sharks can smell one drop of blood from 3 miles (4.8 kilometers) away. Sharks can also sense one drop of blood in a billion drops of water. They have large nostrils on their nose. Their nostrils are not used for breathing, just for smelling.

Pages 14–15

Great white sharks swim when they sleep. Sharks need to keep moving so that water flows over their gills. This keeps oxygen flowing through them. Sharks do not close their eyes when they sleep. They rest one side of their brain at a time in order to get their sleep.

Pages 16–17

Great white sharks grow new teeth all their life. Great white sharks have about 300 sharp, triangular teeth in several rows in their mouths. Their teeth fall out easily and often, and they grow new ones to replace them.

Pages 18–19

Great white sharks can find a heartbeat from 9 feet (2.7 m) away. Sharks have tiny holes in their snouts. These holes lead to canals in their heads that are filled with a kind of jelly. The jelly helps sharks sense electrical currents, including the heartbeats and muscle movements of people and animals.

Pages 20–21

Great white sharks have big fins on their backs. Great white sharks are a vulnerable species. They can get caught in fishing nets and are often killed for their body parts. In some parts of the world, shark fins are used to make soup. There are fewer than 3,500 great white sharks left in the world.

23

WORD LIST

Research has shown that as much as 65 percent of all written material published in English is made up of 300 words. These 300 words cannot be taught using pictures or learned by sounding them out. They must be recognized by sight. This book contains 34 common sight words to help young readers improve their reading fluency and comprehension. This book also teaches young readers several important content words, such as proper nouns. These words are paired with pictures to aid in learning and improve understanding.

Page	Sight Words First Appearance	Page	Content Words First Appearance
4	a, am, great, I, white	4	shark
6	food, in, its, that, the	6	fish, ocean
8	have, like, paper	8	sand, skin
10	any, do, my, not	10	body, bones
12	away, can, from, miles, of, one, three	12	blood, drop
14	when	16	teeth
16	all, grow, life, new	18	beat, heart
18	feet, find	20	fin
20	back, big, on		

Check out av2books.com for activities, videos, audio clips, and more!

 Go to av2books.com

 Enter book code D213883

 Explore your great white shark book!

www.av2books.com